D1710050

ANTLERS AND HORNS

Jason Cooper

Publishing LLC
Vero Beach, Florida 32964

www.rourkepublishing.com

PHOTO CREDITS: All photos © Lynn M. -except pg. 10 © Tom De Bruyne pg. 15 © Sarah Skiba pg. 14 © Philip Puleo

Title page: Bighorn sheep wear thick horns that curl.

Editor: Robert Stengard-Olliges

Cover design by Nicola Stratford.

Library of Congress Cataloging-in-Publication Data

Cooper, Jason
 Antlers and horns / Jason Cooper.
    p. cm. -- (Let's look at animals)
 ISBN 1-60044-168-8 (Hardcover)
 ISBN 1-59515-533-3 (Softcover)
 1. Antlers--Juvenile literature. 2. Horns--Juvenile literature. I.
Title. II. Series: Cooper, Jason. Let's look at animals.
 QL942.S734 2007
 591.47--dc22
                                 2006012743

Printed in the USA

CG/CG

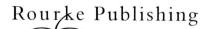

Rourke Publishing

www.rourkepublishing.com – sales@rourkepublishing.com
Post Office Box 3328, Vero Beach, FL 32964

Table of Contents

Animal Hats

Animals do not wear hats. But some wear horns or antlers on their heads.

You can lift a hat off a head. Horns and antlers are different from a hat. Horns and antlers grow from an animal's head!

Two Branches

Antlers spread like the branches of a tree.

Horns do not have branches, except in the **pronghorn.** A pronghorn has **spikes** on each horn.

An animal with horns usually has two. Both **males** and **females** usually have horns. The two horns of an animal are much alike.

8

Animals have horns of different shapes and sizes. They may be straight. They may curl backward. They may have twists. They may grow sideways like a cape buffalo's horns.

Farm Animals, Wild Animals

Farm animals like cattle, goats, and sheep grow horns. Many wild animals have horns. Antelopes, bison, buffaloes, bighorn sheep, and mountain goats are some of the wild animals with horns.

Only deer and their cousins have antlers. Only male deer, moose, and elk normally have antlers. Both male and female **caribou** have antlers.

Antlers Grow Back

Horns stay with an animal for its lifetime. Antlers do not. Animals with antlers lose them each winter.

Each spring antlers begin to grow again.

New antlers are covered by skin and soft hair. New antlers look like they have **velvet** covers!

Under the skin, blood flows to the antlers. The antlers grow large. They grow harder, too. Horns are always hard.

16

By late summer, the velvet peels away. The hard new antlers shine.

Protection

Animals with horns or antlers use them to fight each other. The males fight to find out, which is strongest.

The strongest males gather females. The strongest males keep other males away.

Animals with horns or antlers eat plants. They do not use horns or antlers to kill other animals for food. They will use their horns or antlers to protect themselves.

Glossary

caribou (KA ri boo): a deer of the artic; the wild cousin of reindeer

female (FEE male): girl or mother deer

male (MALE): boy or father deer

pronghorn (PRONG horn): a hoofed and horned animal of the American West

spike (SPIKE): a type of long object with a sharp point

velvet (VEL vit): a type of soft cloth; the covering on new antlers

Index

FURTHER READING

Townsend, Emil. *Deer*. Capstone Press, 2004.

Wheeler, Lisa. *Uncles and Antlers*. Atheneum Books, 2004

WEBSITES TO VISIT

http://www.scsc.k12.ar.us/2001Outwest/PacificEcology/Projects/RoarkJ/Default.htm

http://www.nps.gov/yell/kidstuff/AHgame/ahdiffer.htm

ABOUT THE AUTHOR

Jason cooper has written many children's books for Rourke Publishing about a variety of topics. Cooper travels widely to gather information for his books.